Fun and Simple State Crafts

*Fun and Simple

New England State Crafts

Maine, New Hampshire, Vermont, Massachusetts, Rhode Island, and Connecticut

June Ponte

Enslow Elementary
an imprint of

Enslow Publishers, Inc.
40 Industrial Road
Box 398
Berkeley Heights, NJ 07922
USA

http://www.enslow.com

This book meets the National Council for the Social Studies standards.

Enslow Elementary, an imprint of Enslow Publishers, Inc.

Enslow Elementary® is a registered trademark of Enslow Publishers, Inc.

Library of Congress Cataloging-in-Publication Data

Ponte, June.
    Fun and simple New England state crafts : Maine, New Hampshire, Vermont, Massachusetts,
      Rhode Island, and Connecticut / June Ponte.
      p. cm. — (Fun and simple state crafts)
    Summary: "Provides facts and craft ideas for each of the states that make up the New England
      region of the United States"—Provided by publisher.
    Includes bibliographical references and index.
    ISBN-13: 978-0-7660-2934-7
    ISBN-10: 0-7660-2934-4
    1. Handicraft—New England—Juvenile literature. I. Title.
    TT23.15.P65 2008
    745.50974—dc22

                              2007014029

Printed in the United States of America

10 9 8 7 6 5 4 3 2 1

To Our Readers:
We have done our best to make sure all Internet Addresses in this book were active and appropriate when we went to press. However, the author and the publisher have no control over and assume no liability for the material available on those Internet sites or on other Web sites they may link to. Any comments or suggestions can be sent by e-mail to comments@enslow.com or to the address on the back cover.

Every effort has been made to locate all copyright holders of material used in this book. If any errors or omissions have occurred, corrections will be made in future editions of this book.

♻ Enslow Publishers, Inc., is committed to printing our books on recycled paper. The paper in every book contains 10% to 30% post-consumer waste (PCW). The cover board on the outside of each book contains 100% PCW. Our goal is to do our part to help young people and the environment too!

Illustration Credits: Crafts prepared by June Ponte; Photography by Nicole diMella/Enslow Publishers, Inc.; © 1999 Artville, LLC, pp. 6–7; © 2007 Jupiterimages, all clipart; © 2001 Robesus, Inc., all state flags.

Cover Illustration: Crafts prepared by June Ponte; Photography by Nicole diMella/Enslow Publishers, Inc.; © 2007 Jupiterimages, state buttons; © 1999 Artville, LLC, map.

CONTENTS

WELCOME TO NEW ENGLAND!

Connecticut, Maine, Massachusetts, New Hampshire, Rhode Island, and Vermont are the six states in the New England region. The area was named by Captain John Smith, an English soldier and explorer. Captain Smith explored the Massachusetts Bay area of New England in the early 1600s, and he made a map of the area.

The New England region is in the northeastern part of the United States. Millions of years ago, New England's many mountains and valleys were created by plate collisions, when continental plates collided to form the supercontinent Pangea.

Mount Washington in New Hampshire is the tallest mountain in New England. The Connecticut River is the longest and largest river in New England. It forms the border between Vermont and New Hampshire. Lake Champlain is a long, thin lake, and the largest lake in the region. It lies between Vermont and New York.

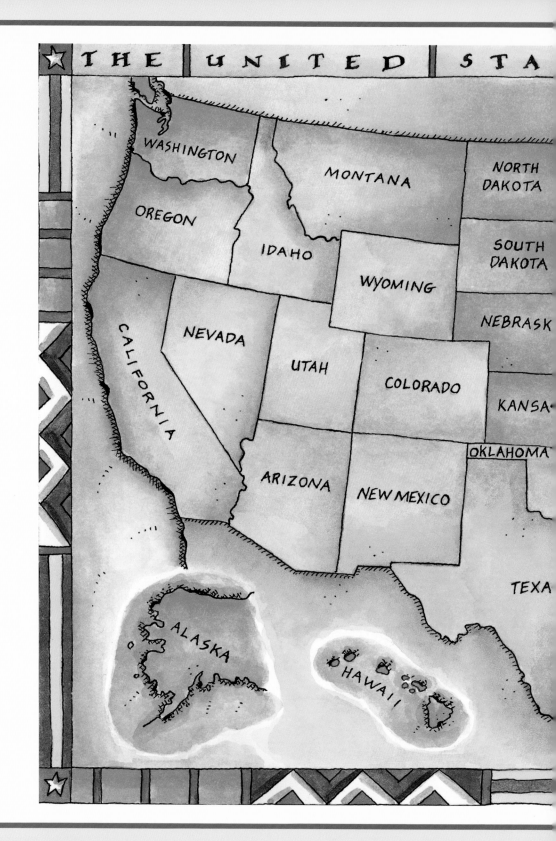

NEW. HAMPSHIRE

MAINE

VERMONT

MINNESOTA

WISCONSIN

MICHIGAN

NEW YORK

MASSACHUSETTS

RHODE ISLAND

IOWA

ILLINOIS

INDIANA

OHIO

PENNSYLVANIA

CONNECTICUT

NEW JERSEY

DELAWARE

MARYLAND

WASHINGTON, D.C.

MISSOURI

WEST VIRGINIA

VIRGINIA

KENTUCKY

NORTH CAROLINA

ARKANSAS

TENNESSEE

SOUTH CAROLINA

MISSISSIPPI

ALABAMA

GEORGIA

LOUISIANA

FLORIDA

N

New England States

MAINE

STATEHOOD 1820

Origin of name	Maine may have been named after a region of France called Mayne. It is also possible that the state was named Maine by explorers, as a shortened version of the word "mainland."
Flag	The Maine state flag is blue, with the state seal in the center. It shows a farmer and a seaman who represent farming and the fishing industry. The shield between them, which has a pine tree and a moose, represents Maine's wildlife regions and forests. The North Star at the top symbolizes Maine's location within the United States.
Capital	Augusta
Nickname	The Pine Tree State

Motto	*Dirigo* (This is Latin for "I direct.")
Size (in area)	39th largest
Animal	moose
Bird	chickadee
Fish	landlocked salmon
Flower	pinecone and tassel from the white pine tree
Tree	white pine
Industry	agriculture, especially potato farming; lumber, shipbuilding, fishing, machinery, electronics, tourism

PAUL BUNYAN STATUE

The town of Bangor, Maine, claims to be where the lumber industry began. Lumber is wood that has been sawed into boards and other pieces for building. People say that Bangor is the place where Paul Bunyan, the legendary lumberjack, was born. There is a 31-foot-tall statue of the tall-tale hero in Bangor. Make a miniature statue of Paul Bunyan.

What you will need

* pipe cleaners
* self-hardening clay
* toothpick (optional)
* toilet tissue tube
* poster paint
* paintbrush
* clear packing tape
* small rock, to fit inside toilet tissue tube
* white glue

What you will do

1. Make the framework for the statue. Twist two pipe cleaners together to make arms. Repeat for legs and a head.

10   Maine

2. Cover the pipe cleaners with clay to form the head, torso, arms, legs, and feet. Let dry. If you like, make an ax. Cover a toothpick with clay, and then add a small rectangle of clay at one end.

3. Make a tree stump that will help the statue stand. Paint a toilet tissue tube brown. Let dry. Cover the bottom of the tube with packing tape. Drop a rock inside the tube to weight it down.

4. Paint a shirt, pants, and boots on the statue. Let dry. Glue the statue to the tree stump toilet tissue tube. Let dry.

My Town Globe

Eartha is the name of the world's largest rotating globe. It is over 41 feet wide. Eartha was made in 1998 by DeLorme, a software company in Maine. Here is a craft in which your town is marked with a star on the globe.

What you will need

* round balloon
* yarn
* flour
* water
* bowl
* strips of newspaper
* poster paint
* paintbrush
* foil star sticker

What you will do

1. Blow up a round balloon. Tie it off. Tie a 24-inch-long piece of yarn around the knot.

2. Mix 1 cup of flour and 2 cups of water in a bowl to make a thin paste. Dip strips of newspaper in

the paste. Use your fingers to wipe off any excess paste. Wrap the strips around the balloon until it is covered with four to five layers of paper. Make sure the yarn is not covered. Let dry overnight.

3. Paint the wrapped balloon to look like a globe. Look at a map or a globe to see the shape of the continents. Let dry. Put a foil star sticker on the globe near where you live.

NEW HAMPSHIRE	
Origin of name	New Hampshire was named after Hampshire, England, by its founder, Captain John Mason. Captain Mason was an English naval officer who received a grant to the land from the Council for New England.
Flag	The New Hampshire state flag is blue. Because New Hampshire was the ninth state to approve the U.S. Constitution, there are nine stars within a laurel wreath on the flag. A Revolutionary War ship, the *Raleigh,* is in the center. The *Raleigh* was built in Portsmouth, New Hampshire.
Capital	Concord

Nickname	The Granite State
Motto	"Live Free or Die"
Size (in area)	46th largest
Animal	white-tailed deer
Bird	purple finch
Fish	brook trout (freshwater) and striped bass (saltwater)
Flower	purple lilac
Tree	white birch
Industry	tourism, high technology, lumber, paper production, folk crafts

STONEHENGE CALENDAR

Stonehenge is an ancient monument in Wiltshire County, England. It is a group of very large stones set in a round pattern. Did you know there is a Stonehenge-like rock structure in North Salem, New Hampshire? Archaeologists, the scientists who study things made by people from the past, are not sure who created this site, or what it was used for. Some people think the markings on the rocks are ancient writing. The site could have been made by people who lived during the Bronze Age, which dates back as far as 4,000 B.C.

What you will need

* 12 small flat rocks
* 1 pointed rock
* permanent black marker
* white glue
* heavy cardboard, 9 inches x 12 inches
* glitter
* poster paint
* paintbrush

During this period, people learned to make tools and weapons from bronze. This rock structure might have been used as a calendar. North Salem's "Stonehenge" could have been made by American Indians or by colonial farmers.

What you will do

A)

1. Collect twelve small flat rocks (See A). Try to find rocks that are somewhat rectangular and similar in size. Find one rock that looks a bit like a triangle. It should be slightly longer and pointier than the others. Wash and dry the rocks so that they are clean and easier to write on.

B)

2. Use a marker to label each rock with a different month of the year. Glue the twelve rocks in a circular shape onto the heavy cardboard. Let dry. Glue glitter on the pointed rock (See B). Let dry. Place the pointed rock in the center of the circle. Paint a design on the cardboard around the circle of rocks. Let dry.

C)

3. Use your Stonehenge calendar by moving the triangular rock to point toward the current month (See C).

CASTLE

Did you know there is a real castle in Moultonborough, New Hampshire? Thomas Gustave Plant was a very rich man who wanted to live in a place where he could see only beauty. His castle, called *Lucknow*, was built in 1914, and is on 6,300 acres of land. If you could build your own castle, what would it look like?

What you will need

* small box
* paintbrush
* poster paint
* colored cellophane or plastic wrap
* scissors
* white glue
* construction paper
* glitter pen
* self-hardening clay

What you will do

1. Paint the outside of the small box gray (See A).

2. Cut out windows and doors. Cut out colored cellophane or plastic wrap and glue to the inside of the castle windows. Let dry. You can draw bricks or stones on the castle walls if you

A)

like, or decorate the castle with glitter. On construction paper, make a sign with your name that fits over the door, such as, "Tom's Castle" (See B).

3. What would you like in your castle? Use clay to make little people, furniture, or whatever you can imagine. Let dry overnight. Paint your clay items and let dry.

4. Place the objects inside and outside of your castle, and have fun (See C)!

B)

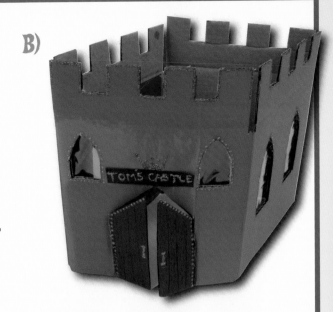

C)

VERMONT

Origin of name	Vermont received its name from the French words *vert mont*, which means "green mountain."
Flag	Vermont's state flag is blue. In the center of the flag is Vermont's official symbol, or coat of arms. It shows a pine tree, grain, and a cow, with mountains in the background.
Capital	Montpelier
Nickname	The Green Mountain State

20

Motto	"Freedom and Unity"
Size (in area)	45th largest
Animal	Morgan horse
Bird	hermit thrush
Fish	brook trout (cold water) and walleye pike (warm water)
Flower	red clover
Tree	sugar maple
Industry	paper manufacture, lumber, maple syrup, dairy farming, tourism, electronics

CHAMP, THE LAKE MONSTER

For many years, people have reported seeing unusual looking creatures in Vermont lakes. Legend has it that Lake Champlain and Lake Memphremagog both have lake monsters swimming in them! Champ is the name of the lake monster from Lake Champlain while Memphre is the name given to the creature in Lake Memphremagog. Champ was called "Tatoskok" by the Abenaki American Indians who lived near the lake. People say that Champ and Memphre look like long-necked dinosaurs.

What you will need

* light blue and cream construction paper
* pencil
* scissors
* glitter pen
* markers
* wiggle eye
* white glue
* craft stick

What you will do

1. Draw an oval on blue construction paper. (See page 46 for the pattern.) Cut out the oval.

A)

2. In the middle of the oval, draw a wavy line. Cut along the wavy line (See A).

3. Use markers and glitter to add detail and more waves. Draw some fish or other sea life (See B).

4. Draw a lake monster on cream-colored construction paper. (See page 45 for the pattern.) Cut it out.

B)

5. Glue a wiggle eye on the lake monster. Draw a mouth with a glitter pen. Let dry. Turn the lake monster over, and glue the end of the craft stick to the end of the body (See C). Let dry.

6. Slide the lake monster through the wave slit in the lake (See D). Move the craft stick and watch Champ swim!

C)

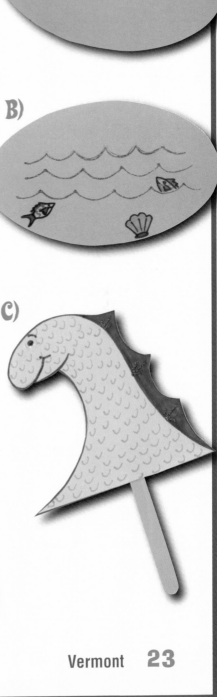

D)

SNOWFLAKE TREASURE BOX

Wilson A. "Snowflake" Bentley was a Vermont farmer. He was the first person to take a picture of a single snowflake crystal. Bently took photographs of more than 5,000 snowflakes, and never found two that were alike. He became known as the Snowflake Man.

What you will need

* blue, light blue, purple, and white construction paper
* pencil
* scissors
* shoe box
* aluminum foil
* clear tape
* white glue
* water
* bowl
* paintbrush
* glitter pens

What you will do

1. Draw twelve circles, three on each color of construction paper. (See page 46 for the pattern.) Cut out the circles.

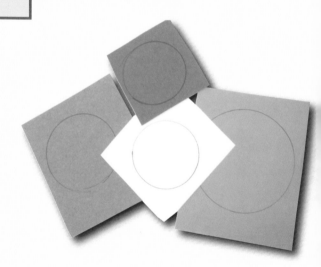

A)

2. Fold each circle in half. Fold them into quarters, and then eighths (See A).

3. Cut little shapes on the folded edge (See B). Carefully cut along the rounded edge. Open all the circles, and see your snowflakes!

B)

4. Cover a shoe box and the shoe box lid with foil (See C). Tape the edges of the foil in place. Glue the snowflakes on the lid of the shoe box (See D). Let them overlap a little bit. Mix 1/4 cup of glue with 1/4 cup of water to make a glue wash. Coat the top of the box with glue wash and let dry. Accent the box with glitter pens. Repeat the process for the sides of the box (See E).

C)

E)

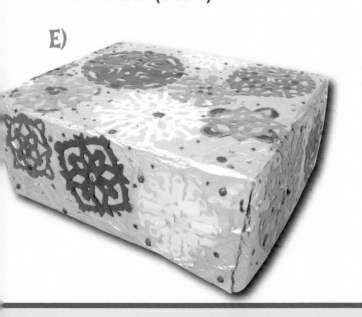

D)

MASSACHUSETTS

Origin of name	Massachusetts was named after the American Indian tribe that lived in the area. The American Indian word *Massachusetts* means "a large hill place."
Flag	The Massachusetts state flag is white. An American Indian is shown with a bow and arrow within a blue shield in the center of the flag. There is a star above the American Indian. It symbolizes Massachusetts as one of the thirteen colonies that later became the first states. Above the shield is an arm holding a sword. This represents the state motto, "By the sword we seek peace, but peace only under liberty."
Capital	Boston

Nickname	**The Old Colony State and The Bay State**
Motto	***Ense petit placidam sub libertate quietem*** **(This is a Latin phrase which means "By the sword we seek peace, but peace only under liberty.")**
Size (in area)	**44th largest**
Animal	**Morgan horse**
Bird	**black-capped chickadee**
Fish	**Atlantic cod**
Flower	**mayflower**
Tree	**American elm**
Industry	**tourism, machinery, electric equipment, scientific instruments, printing, publishing**

Silly Character Statue

The Dr. Seuss National Memorial Sculpture Garden is in Massachusetts at the Springfield Museum. Springfield was the hometown of Theodor Seuss Geisel, known as Dr. Seuss. He wrote books for children and created many memorable characters like the *Cat in the Hat* and *Yertle the Turtle*.

What you will need

* self-hardening clay
* wiggle eyes
* white glue
* poster paint
* paintbrush
* craft feathers or cotton balls

What you will do

1. Use a piece of clay that is about 4 inches long and 2 inches wide to create any shape you wish. This silly character can look any way you would like. Use your

imagination to make your very own funny character that no one has ever seen before! Let clay dry overnight.

2. Glue on wiggle eyes. Paint the character as you wish. Let dry. Glue on craft feathers or stretched out cotton balls for hair.

3. Display your character. What other silly characters can you make?

JOHNNY APPLESEED PLANTER

John Chapman grew up in the Massachusetts town of Leominster in the late 1700s. He left home when he was a teenager, and became a legend for spreading apple seeds throughout the Ohio Valley. He became known as Johnny Appleseed. There are still cider mills and apple orchards in Leominster that people say had their beginnings from Johnny Appleseed's work.

What you will need

* pint-sized milk or juice carton
* scissors
* brown construction paper
* clear tape
* green, red, and yellow foam or construction paper
* green tissue paper
* soil
* apple seeds

What you will do

1. Cut off the top of a clean pint-sized carton (See A).

2. Cut a piece of brown construction paper that is as tall as the carton,

A)

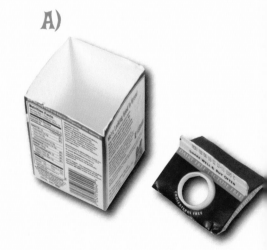

and long enough to wrap around it. Tape the construction paper tightly around the carton (See B).

B)

3. Cut two red apples, one green apple, and one yellow apple from craft foam or construction paper. (See page 44 for the pattern) (See C).

C)

4. Glue one apple to each side of the carton. Cut out eight green tissue paper leaves. (See page 44 for the pattern.) Glue two leaves to the top of each apple (See D).

5. Fill the carton with soil. Push the apple seeds 2 inches deep into the soil (See E). Keep the soil moist but not wet. In about a month, you should see your apple tree seedling.

D)

E)

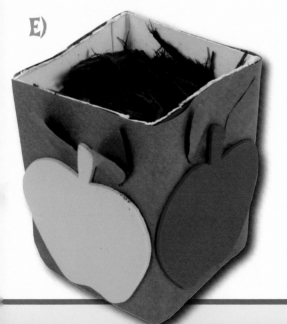

(apple seeds)

RHODE ISLAND

Origin of name	Some say Rhode Island was named by Adrian Block, a Dutch explorer. He called it *Roodt Eylandt*, which means "Red Island." Block was thought to have named the state after the red clay he found there. Others believe Rhode Island was named for the Greek island, Rhodes.
Flag	The Rhode Island state flag is white. Thirteen gold stars surround an anchor in the center of the flag. The stars represent the original thirteen colonies. On a blue ribbon below the anchor is the word "Hope," Rhode Island's state motto.
Capital	Providence

Nickname	Little Rhody, and The Ocean State
Motto	"Hope"
Size (in area)	50th largest
Bird	Rhode Island red chicken
Fish	striped bass
Flower	violet
Tree	red maple
Industry	electronic equipment, wire, glassware and jewelry, high technology, finance

GREEN ANIMALS TOPIARY GARDEN

There are eighty unusually shaped trees at the Green Animals Topiary Garden in Rhode Island. Topiary trees are trees that are shaped into the forms of animals or other objects. There are twenty-one animal topiary trees at the garden, including an elephant, rooster, teddy bear, giraffe, and unicorn.

What you will need

* small round balloon
* bowl
* flour
* water
* newspaper strips
* green poster paint
* paintbrush
* toilet tissue tube
* scissors
* white glue
* green tissue paper
* wiggle eyes

What you will do

1. Blow up the balloon, and tie it tightly. Mix 1 cup of flour and 3 cups of water in a bowl to make a thin paste. Dip strips of newspaper in the paste. Wipe off any excess with your fingers. Wrap the strips around the balloon until it is covered with four to five layers of paper (See A). Let dry overnight.

2. Paint the balloon green (See B). Let dry.

3. Flatten the toilet tissue tube. Cut four 1/2-inch round pieces for the legs (See C). Glue the legs to the balloon. Let dry. Cut one 1/2-inch round piece for the snout. Glue the snout to the balloon. Let dry.

4. Tear pieces of green tissue paper into strips (See D). Glue the tissue paper on the balloon. Glue on the wiggle eyes. Paint the legs and snout green (See E). Let dry.

A)

B)

E)

C)

D)

BIG BUG

Yikes! The world's largest bug is on top of the New England Pest Control building in Providence, Rhode Island. It is a big blue termite named Nibbles Woodaway. Some people just call it the Big Blue Bug, because it is 58 feet long!

What you will need

* self-hardening clay
* six black bobby pins
* cotton swabs
* scissors
* paintbrush
* poster paint
* small wiggle eyes
* white glue

What you will do

1. Make three egg-shaped pieces from clay (See A).

2. Carefully join them together. Blend the clay together until the three pieces are joined.

A)

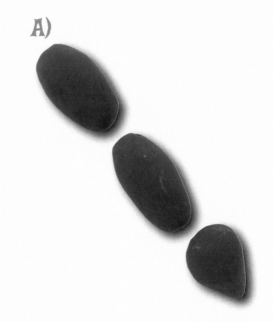

3. Gently push the open end of two bobby pins into the left and right side of each body segment (See B).

4. Cut a cotton swab in half. Paint with black poster paint (See C). Let dry.

5. Gently push the cotton swabs into the bug's head. Let the clay harden overnight. Paint as you wish. Let dry. Glue wiggle eyes on the head (See D). Let dry.

B)

C)

D)

CONNECTICUT

Origin of name	The name *Connecticut* comes from the American Indian word *quinnehtukqut*, which means "place beside a long river."
Flag	The Connecticut state flag is blue. A gold shield is in the center of the flag with grapevines on it. The grapevines represent the original colonists who came to the area from Europe.
Capital	Hartford
Nickname	The Nutmeg State and The Constitution State

Motto	*Qui transtulit sustinet* (This is a Latin phrase which means "he who transplanted still sustains.")
Size (in area)	48th largest
Animal	sperm whale
Bird	American robin
Fish	American shad
Flower	mountain laurel
Tree	white oak
Industry	chemical products, scientific instruments, transportation equipment

WILD PARAKEET IN NEST

Monk parakeets are found in the wild in South America. Some bird experts believe that crates of these birds were broken at Kennedy Airport in New York. The birds, which were to be sold as pets, flew away. Now, colorful Monk parakeets live in nests they build in trees near the coast of Connecticut. You can make a model of a Monk parakeet.

What you will need

* self-hardening clay
* yellow pipe cleaners
* poster paint
* paint brush
* 2 craft feathers for wings (optional)
* white glue
* 2 small wiggle eyes
* 20 to 30 thin twigs, about 6 inches long

What you will do

1. For the body, mold a piece of clay into an egg shape. For the head, mold another piece of clay into a smaller egg shape (See A).

2. Squeeze and flatten one end of the large egg-shaped clay to form a tail. Add a

A)

B)

small piece of clay to the smaller egg-shaped piece to form a beak (See B).

3. Using a yellow pipe cleaner, make three toes by bending sections of the pipe cleaner in half three times (See C). Wrap a pipe cleaner around the foot twice to keep the toes in the right shape. The remaining pipe cleaner forms the leg. Cut the pipe cleaner so the leg measures 3 inches long. Repeat to make a second leg.

C)

4. Push the legs 1 inch deep into the bottom of the parakeet's body. Carefully squeeze the clay tightly around the bird's legs. Let the clay dry. Paint the bird using poster paint. Let dry. If you wish, glue on wiggle eyes and craft feathers for wings (See D). Let dry.

5. Glue thin twigs together to make a nest for the bird. Let it dry. Place the parakeet in his new home (See E)!

D)

E)

LOLLIPOP CANDY CHEST

George Smith was a candy maker in the early 1900s. He thought putting hard candy on a stick would make it easier to eat. He named the candy after his favorite racing horse, Lolly Pop. In 1908, one of the first lollipop machines was making forty lollipops per minute in Smith's shop. How about making your own special lollipop candy chest?

What you will need

* small cardboard box with flip-up lid, such as an herbal tea box
* cream-colored construction paper
* pencil
* scissors
* glitter pen
* colored cellophane or plastic wrap
* white glue
* pipe cleaners in different colors
* markers
* lollipops

What you will do

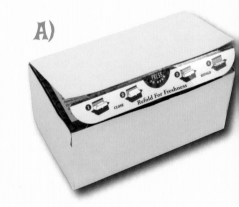

A)

1. Trace the sides and top of the cardboard box onto cream-colored construction paper and cut out. Glue the paper to the box (See A). Let dry.

Write "Lollipop Candy Chest" on the front of the box using a glitter pen.

2. Cut out six small circles from the colored cellophane or plastic wrap (See B). Cut six small pieces of pipe cleaners. Glue the circles to the top and sides of the box. Glue small pipe cleaners to the circles as the "lollipop sticks." Let dry. Use markers to draw little lollipops in between the big lollipops (See C).

3. Fill the candy chest with lollipops to share with your friends!

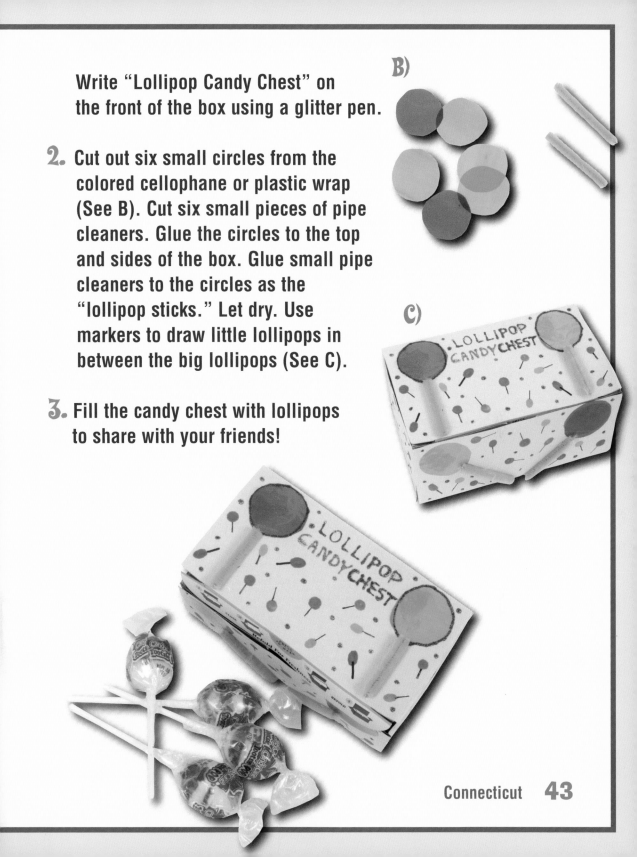

B)

C)

PATTERNS

Use tracing paper to copy the patterns on these pages. Ask an adult to help you cut and trace the shapes.

Johnny Appleseed Planter

At 100%

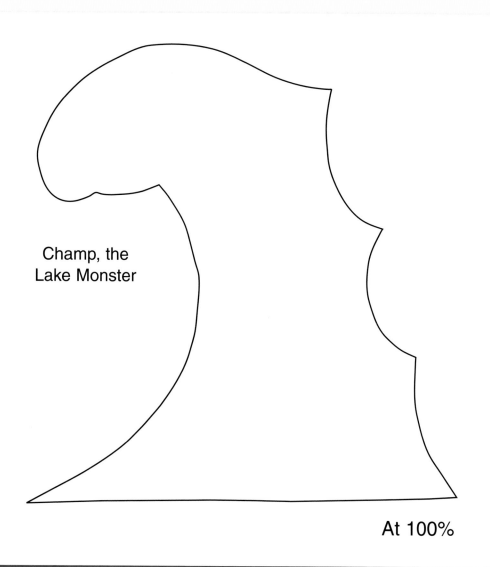

Champ, the
Lake Monster

At 100%

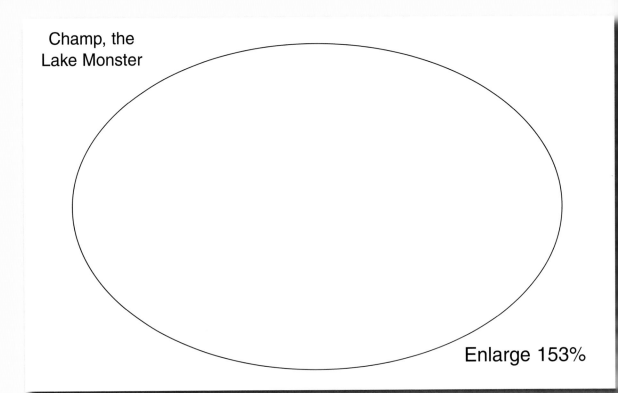

Champ, the
Lake Monster

Enlarge 153%

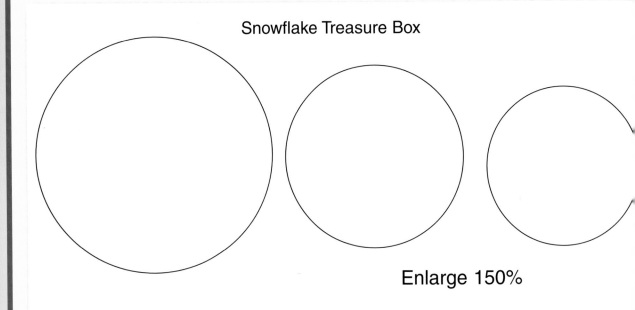

Snowflake Treasure Box

Enlarge 150%

LEARN MORE

Books

Bjorklund, Ruth. *Massachusetts.* New York: Benchmark Books, 2003.

Dubois, Muriel L. *New Hampshire: Facts and Symbols.* Mankato, Minn.: Capstone Press, 2003.

Heinrichs, Ann. *Rhode Island.* Minneapolis, Minn.: Compass Point Books, 2004.

McAuliffe, Emily. *Connecticut: Facts and Symbols.* Mankato, Minn.: Capstone Press, 2003.

Pelta, Kathy. *Vermont.* Minneapolis, Minn.: Lerner Publications, 2002.

Webster, Christine. *Maine.* New York: Children's Press, 2003.

Internet Addresses

50states.com
<http://www.50states.com/>

U.S. States
<http://www.enchantedlearning.com/usa/states/>

INDEX